THE BOO

Lo! thy dread empire, CHAOS! is restor'd;
Light dies before thy uncreating word

—ALEXANDER POPE, *The Dunciad*

Contents

ONE

The Book of Revelation

'I am the Alpha and the Omega,' says the Lord God, 'who is,
and who was, and who is to come, the Almighty.' (v.8)

Somewhere off-calendar, beyond the powergrub annals,
neither alpha nor omega, L-plated, No oned, rubble M,
immoderate in extremis, no *gloria in excelsis* I sing, O
far-off God of lampstand and practised anglepoise,
stars flaring on your palm: fiery balm to cigarette
bearers of light unto death, a last puff of smoke
begun with first gasp. If everything connects,
nothing connects; not the was and is and is
to come, not the architecture of a human
brain – that divine ur-studio clodpiece
running CloudCuckooLand on broken
biscuits and Laa-Laa lobes. Nothing
matters if all of it matters more
or less equally to everybody.
No matter! Mark the epoch
of lips and tits. Which are
more popular with your
target group? Or mark
the apocalypse with
twats on Twitter,
you decide! The
people have
spoken. By

refer end
dumdum
dum di
dum
du
d

Chapter 2

'I know your deeds, your love and faith, your service and
perseverance, and that you are now doing more than you did at
first. Nevertheless, I have this against you . . .' (vv.19–20)

I know your works, but hold this against you:
something murmured many years ago, under
influence of the Totaleitans, and forgotten
until that time when all will be revealed

among the barbarous elect: medicinal
dogmatics, delivered with coffin-bearing
slapstick, to answer questions never asked
except in ancient, sponsored muttering:

how they snapped Elastic Man, why no X-
mas for monkeys, what always remains
breakable among the already broken:
battered shards, burned out words,

the preservation of a foetus's potential
to bear arms and blast bullets through
soft matter: skin, brains, lack of rigour.
How easy it is to feel opposed, and yet

do their bidding only to receive a white
stone, a gateway to the second death;
unwillingly covet authority over nations,
Mammon, the nodding, morning star.

[5]

CHAPTER 3

'I know your deeds, that you are neither cold nor hot.
I wish you were either one or the other!' (v.15)

My emails to a capybara win the Ted Hughes Award:
I now stand accused of plagiarising the Philadelphian
Epistle and random lyrics from The Fall, some bootleg
from *Totale's Turn*. But I'll never never never never

copy again, so that's OK. After each award ceremony,
Ted's coffin sinks a little deeper into the Inferno's
floodlit semicircle of shame. Its door is always open
and no one will remove the pay-by-view binoculars

pinned on every coned face. Our thoughts and prayers
are with them, even though we never actually pray
or think. Ted's last poem was called *The Thought Fuck*
and involves neither thinking nor fucking. Try Praying;

I should have prayed for a Creative Scotland grant
to write in situ, perched on Patmos rock and recording
local detail at taxpayers' expense: how other poets –
the true professionals – wangle a holiday from doing

nothing at all except scribbling in sand, what I do when
neither working nor plagiarising. My guinea pig poems
are just plagiarised capybaras. The reviews maintain
Mark E. Smith was just the John of Patmos of his day.

A poet ridicules a review of his collection: the woman
reviewer is clannish, autophobic, irascibly incorrect
and confuses pronouns with paradelles. Better that
than lukewarm, blowing neither hot nor cold, I say,

and recommend a quezalcoatlus northropi as emotional
support for future odyssey. In the Kingdom of Extinction,
a stuffed dinosaur takes wing. Like a prehistoric crow
it screams, 'Mackenzie, I spit you out of my mouth!'

CHAPTER 4

*From the throne came flashes of lightning, rumblings and peals of
thunder. In front of the throne, seven lamps were blazing. (v.5)*

I almost miss night clubs at closing time
                    when staff light the lamps, and lines
            appear, dramatized, on wincing faces

that fade into sleep. No one told me about
                    heaven's obsession with insomnia,
            its ubiquitous floodlight revivalists:

Brighten the corners! Blight the dawn!
                    The merest celestial pavement gleam
            serves to dim each memory of worldly

form and brilliance. Unlike the legendary
                    northern dusk, the bulbs will never
            explode, the songs will never fade out.

Absence of shadow, eyes everywhere,
                    panoramic vision; nothing remains
            hidden except, shielded in brightness,

everything. Who can gaze upon the face
                    of God and live? The night bus is gaudy
            with 5D video ringtones, the volume

impertinently maximum. No wonder Milton
              captured cinereal duplicities in darkness
          sharper than heaven's screenshot tablets:

What hath night to do with sleep? A question
              night after night the sleepless repeat –
          blue screen winking; the power of negative

bunk to bunk blue funk thinking results
              in over-exposure; nightmarecap Barolo
          cups run over to fuel the tawny sewer

with uberneon tannin. I have not slept
              and eternity is worth the time only while
          endings and awakenings are possible.

CHAPTER 5

'Who is worthy to break the seals and open the scroll?' (v.2)

The lion has triumphed.
I saw a lamb, struck,
looking as if it had been slain,
able to open the seven seals.

Why does God, a bowl
without crack – a golden
bowl – hide in cracks,
in things we don't know?

I believe in my own twaddle.
Otherwise, I might fairly
have been amused by
the great gold cup.

'Love is perfect when imperfect.'
I'm happy with my oily words
and unseen miracles we must
somehow drain together.

There is no assignment of
incense bowls. I feel the day
like a cloud of half-promises:
each one we may perish by.

CHAPTER 6

The sky receded like a scroll, rolling up. (v.14)

Hear what has been written, and then unwritten:
hoofmark glyphs the rain translates into
schmaltz. Here come the sentimental gutter-
snoops with photography in mind

for hoofmark glyphs their spin translates
into dance routines by plastic rocking horses.
Snipes, with cryptography in mind,
beat out sarcastic drumrolls overhead.

Dance routines by Nazi rocking horses
belie illusion. The liberal cognoscenti
threaten the cast with dumbbells to the head,
breathe hymns to little stalins everywhere.

Defy illusion! The liberal egocentrics
feed on slogans, while microscopic hitlers
hymn death with little stalins everywhere.
'Relax,' they say, 'The pale rider means well.'

Beyond the slogans, trite biopic hitlers
fake news. As true as feels no different.
Death, the pale rider, comes out of his shell.
The sky falls as one starlit scroll and, look!

Fake news or true? Can you tell the difference?
See what has been written, and then unwritten:
the sky folds into a vapid scroll, the Book
of Schmaltz. Here comes the sentimental gutter.

CHAPTER 7

Then I heard the number of those who were sealed: 144,000. (v.4)

Everyone knows Di Caprio and Winslet made the Titanic
what it was, that history abandoned the great multitude
in one wave from Celine Dion's folding, ship-shaped fan.

My art will go on! Sound of the freshly lionized in panic
at feline neon-lit names eulogized in flattening platitudes.
Another ship sunk. Artists navigate their own extinction.

I fire potshots at my feted self from the palatial margin.

CHAPTER 8

*... a third of the sun was struck, a third of the moon, and a third
of the stars, so that a third of them turned dark. A third of the
day was without light, and also a third of the night.* (v.12)

A third want duty without responsibility,
a third the opposite; the latter become
cabinet ministers and amateur foragers.
The remaining third cling to a mythical
middle ground, blunder down either path
without knowing it. A third of the earth
is burned up, and a third of the trees.
Every green flare of grass is burned up.
A third of words are needlessly repeated;
two thirds of published poems are unread
except by their authors; almost a third
not even by them. Two thirds of experts
establish a synonym between Farage
and cabbage; one third is a soft rhyme,
a wee beige jobby of Napoleonic lineage.
A third of all statistics are fabricated
like this one; a third approach truth in
extreme conditions, like an inch of snow
south of Birmingham; a third suggest
nefarious purpose and will often add
successive thirds to defy mathematics
and multiply into further long divisions.
A third do things by halves, a third
triple up and ride their identity crisis.

A third of the sea is blood, a third
of fish are clobbered, a third of ships
batter the rocks and lose their war
with surface luminosities before
descending to the depths. A third
follow them; a third follow the sun,
erupt like mushrooms from within.
The star called Wormwood falls on
a third of rivers; a third of waters
fall bitter; a third of the *vox populi*
fall silent and worship bitterness.
A third is nothing, the cynics crow,
but a third of history worth making
seems, to one third of respondents,
to come *ex nihilo* (except in English);
a third think history a waste of time,
when nothing happens, and resign.
A third subscribe to pie-in-the-sky
thinking; a third think its opposite
is toad-in-the-hole; a third think up
many reasons to reimagine the world.

CHAPTER 9

. . . out of the smoke locusts came down on the earth and
were given power like that of scorpions (v.3)

My coffee machine has broken and meanwhile
people share a meme bonding Ishtar and Easter
and take offence at me pointing out the obvious
lack of connection. I am cranky without coffee
but not the kind of crank who cobbles an etymology
from Uruk to Truro, from Mesopotamia to messy
pot mania. I tidy my kitchen and extend the line
of periphrastic cleaners, five millennia of polish
and prolix from Sumeria to Scotland. Meanwhile
the laws of war have been broken and we must
bomb what remains of the cities to uphold them.
World leaders and their armies are just insects
flipped on their backs, says a would-be-viral flop.
Plus ça change, bombs act smart and the more
we enter Memewhile, half-formed bodystacks
teetering on the tipping point of Anapodoton,
plus c'est la même chose. In profile, mean
locust Emperor Apollyon is one third scorpion,
one third lion, but dominant horsey genes
suggest an inner Windsor princess. Presentation
is never entirely ours to control (or was that
'out of control'?); countless hours are wasted
trying to tame our resolute inner cranks.

CHAPTER 10

I was about to write: and I heard a voice from heaven saying unto me, 'Seal up those things which the seven thunders uttered, and write them not.' (v.4)

¹And I saw another mighty angel come down from heaven, clothed with a cloud: and a rainbow was upon his head, and his face was as it were the sun, and his feet as pillars of fire: ²And he had in his hand a little book open: and he set his right foot upon the sea, and his left foot on the earth, ³And cried with a loud voice, as when a lion roareth: and when he had cried, seven thunders uttered their voices. ⁴And when the seven thunders had uttered their voices, I was about to write: and I heard a voice from heaven saying unto me, Seal up those things which the seven thunders uttered, and write them not. . . ¹⁰And I took the little book out of the angel's hand, and ate it up; and it was in my mouth sweet as honey: and as soon as I had eaten it, my belly was bitter.

I saw   th r   a   w   n
     with   cloud and   rain   a
face   as   sun and   feet as pillars of fire
                               book open
          on the sea and   on   earth   And
          lo   v   e as   a lion roareth
d   ie   s   under   their voices
        under ha   t red   s   u   r e
   I hear   voice   s   Seal up
                          un   utter   write them not
. . .   book   of   s   and
             t   a in   t sweet as
          my   bi te

I saw
            l   and
                                d   e   s   ire

            the sea
                        as   a li   e
d   ie   s
      under   a   t   r   u   e
      ear
                                                write them   . . .

                        t   weet
            m   e

I saw

        the
              li   e
    s
          t   e
e r
               t he

       t   weet

w

          e
                    li   e

    r
                              e

        t   weet

li

t   e

CHAPTER 11

'I will give power to my two witnesses, and they will
prophecy for 1,260 days, clothed in sackcloth.' (v.3)

The people bartered gifts
and partied in the streets.
The prophets were dead!

An example to everyone:
their flesh left in a trough
below the National Arch.

We turned away to fill
crackers (or was it cavities?)
and milk battery calves

into macaroni pies. We went
cuckoo for three nights
and the bodies have gone.

Some say crows hoiked them
limb by limb to high nests
to feed a yawning hunger;

some allege burials in gravel
stadia; others feel plagued
by mystery's momentum:

the ease with which myth
can hood itself in sackcloth
and sound as much like truth

as hymn, poem or novel;
the ease of being less alive
when living than in death.

'. . . but woe to the earth and the sea, because the devil has gone down to
you! He is filled with fury, because he knows that his time is short.' (v.12)

The devil is in the hand; a devil
in hand is worth ten in the wish.
The hand never lends a hand,
never gets its finger out, except
to laser Jesus-heads on your
corned beef paté or trace a leak
of milk from the stone Madonna's
chipped nipple. It starts a scene
and leaves a riot. While the quiet
play footsie with the modest,
the devil never holds back from
handstanding on ceremony;
he hands out scraps of advice
to autocrats on strict metrical
forms of population control
and spontaneous handclap.
The hand develops a shake
as weapon, the grip of caffeine;
the devil is also in the decaf,
the details and lack of detail.
It has become hard to identify
the devil in the passably eligible,
who no longer leave the innocent
unhooded to face horn and pitchfork
and, with a tail's hammer, bounce

a third of stars from the night sky.
They operate by stealth and obvious
stupidity, remain obstinate amid
labyrinthine self-contradiction.
Their hands press your buttons.
They multiply, thrive on lack
of recognition, feed on attention.
These hands are hard to handle.
When you switch off the lamp
and when you switch it on again
legions fist-pump in plain sight.

CHAPTER 13

Because of the signs [the second beast] was given power to do on behalf
of the first beast, he deceived the inhabitants of the earth (v.14)

I blessed the president. He called me a bampot,
which I was. He reprised his 'rivers of blood'
TEDx talk and wrapped his car around a lamppost
at maximum speed. He hoped I understood

his metaphorical triple negative and, of course,
I can't say I didn't not. He wasn't the real president,
just a version from a 'literal' translation, which
besides being oxymoronic or perhaps just plain

moronic, made me feel that, yes, I was being
cheated into demonstrating against disappointingly
inauthentic authority; as if what comes *after* Dante,
after Shakespeare, *after* Baudelaire, *after* Pessoa,

is only second-hand murk, inviolably liquid. It must
not be drunk too deeply, although the president
is hardly an advert for temperance. Seriously,
he claimed on YouTube that The Strokes ripped off

Television, but everyone is influenced: chefs who
eat nothing but tinned carbs, and visual artists who
never look at anything, end up with the same
still life pot of spaghetti. You might have heard

the president ordered sickles for the fascists,
missed a business lunch with his rival bottom-
feeder, Simeon the Stylite, shook a walking-stick
at some pussy in a wheelchair and said later

he'd thought it was a magic wand. One third
believed it; one third never believe anything;
one third seemed aware that they ought
at least to check for proof, and some did.

CHAPTER 14

So he who was seated on the cloud swung his sickle over
the earth, and the earth was harvested. (v.16)

Harvest Sunday: sermon lauded the flood,
rainbow oiled a puddle. A hose dropped
petrol in the wineglass. Hogweed instead
of cork hogged the fields of bottletop.

Rotting fruit covered the red carpet above
the chancel steps with offerings of string
and weathered packaging. This was love's
dim twin making sacred, useless things.

The rivers ran with blood and the trains ran
on thought; I could have stopped them any time.
The world tailspun to the sluicing of my brain.
When love came to shove, I pushed a hymn
in praise of shove-love. O, forgive me, Father,
I have sunned in raintime, rained on summer.

CHAPTER 15

They held harps given them by God and sang the song of Moses (vv.2–3)

Long before Carlisle discovered heaven
is a place on earth, thrill-seekers found it
on hilltops and by-the-hour hotel rooms.
But I conduct the true choirs of paradise:
the choristers a billion Mark E. Smiths,
each a little out of tune with all the others
like guitars on the first Buzzcocks album.

I understand such immutable trappings
of afterlife may not satisfy everyone.
There are complaints I admit nothing
chartbound, nothing anyone wants
beyond harps to mollify conventional
expectation. I'd rather cancel eternity
than listen to a democratic jukebox.

So, we each take part alone, knowing
only a personal heaven and insulated
from taste by soundproof earphones.
No leaky drum machines. No interruption!
In prisons of choice, freedom to intrude
spoils the spell. This creed is the social
paradox of heaven, always on repeat,

and I want to tell those girls to switch off
that Drake video they're blasting around
the 22 bus and introduce the theological
concept that freedom's essential value
is realised by curtailing it, but somehow
I know that won't work. Gill says I should
dance on the seats if it happens again –

try at least to tolerate the thoughtless
or I'll end up alone in a high-rise flat,
my naked body face down, contorted on
a polypropylene rug, flanked by single
malt and Irn Bru empties. Sometimes
that sounds like heaven compared to
trying to love enemies and their music.

CHAPTER 16

I heard a loud voice from the temple saying to the seven angels,
'Go, pour out the seven bowls of God's wrath'. (v.1)

The angels spill their tortures on our soil:
boils like hot coals, corpse blood, blood springs, sunstroke,
hush dark, washed-up spirits, earthquake and hail –

nothing more than we are able to endure
or so they say. It's unfair, all the stick
they get. We'll persevere, until we're pure –

pure enough not to shudder when You speak.

CHAPTER 17

This title was written on her forehead:
MYSTERY.
BABYLON THE GREAT.
THE MOTHER OF PROSTITUTES
AND OF THE ABOMINATIONS OF THE EARTH. (v. 5)

Reese Witherspoon wants me. I must choose
a book from a list of recommended thumbnails
and join her Hello Sunshine club. One title is
This Is How It Always Is. And it is. It is just
impossible and all the covers look like they've
targeted the same market: me! It is like trying
to pick a mother. Between the abominations,
prostitutes and mysteries, almost identical
at first glance, I wonder what choice I have.
My genes are too constricting. I must belt up or
self-identify. I'll try self-negation if all else fails
to make a mark. I'll short-circuit the mother-
board of everything I am and do. The mother
of all bottles, puddles, battles, poodles, has me
bark in the dark and follow some yellow brick
motherfucker to Goodbye City or Elton Towers
or Babylon Burning. With the anxiety of one
who neither toils nor spins but fattens on ready
meals, I consider the lilies and the likelihood
that I am just a lukewarm form of abomination,
and that my mother could be everyone-and-his-
mother or mother country or mum's the word
when silence is no option. O Reese, O Oprah,

your taste is impeccable. I am seduced easily
by suggestion, by the books the beast feeds
the bonfire, rousing the flames of middlebrow
hope as a dress rehearsal for extreme times.

CHAPTER 18

Every sea captain, and all who travel by ship, the sailors,
and all who earn their living from the sea, will stand far off.
When they see the smoke of her burning, they will exclaim,
'Was there ever a city like this great city?' (vv.17b–18)

When I cooked beef bourguignon
the burning began in oven time;

when bells rang and clocks awoke
the primary ingredient was smoke

and that smoke hung in judgement
over Edinburgh like a black stain

eclipsing my stainless dress, the one
I bought from the Muriel Spark Store

of Combustible Thoughts, which rage
against lightness with the light touch

of smoke, brief aphorisms briefing
the sky, and the stones will cry out

'Was there ever a sight like this
great sight?' My heart and brain

have turned to stone, but cry
in solidarity with everything

melting or gone, all the while wired
to admire a good bonfire, its gospel

of incineration: scorched earth,
smouldering hen-parties silenced

by noise complaints in the capital;
the befuddlement of a vanished God

insufficiently fashionable to quench
a flame. Was there ever a city,

was there ever? Was there? Was
was the tense of smoke, risen like

truth, blinding truth, truth so dark
that lies will fall lighter on the city.

CHAPTER 19

I saw an angel standing in the sun, who cried in a loud voice to all the birds flying in mid-air, 'Come, gather together for the great supper of God, so that you may eat the flesh of kings, generals and mighty men, of horses and their riders, and the flesh of all people, free and slave, great and small.' (vv.17–18)

The Mob be with you
and also with you.

May the Mob have mercy.
May we have mercy on the Mob.

Lift up your hearts.
The smoke rises for ever and ever.

Blessed is he who trends in the name of the Mob.
He has a name written on him that no one knows but himself.

May we follow the birds tweeting to the air;
out of their beaks come sharp swords.

Spirit of the Mob, you silence dissent.
May the monsters be cast to the burning sulphur.

We break this bread:
the flesh of all people, free and slave, great and small.

Take, eat; these are their bodies, broken for you.
All the birds gorged themselves on their flesh.

CHAPTER 20

Then death and Hades were thrown into the lake of fire. The lake of
fire is the second death. Anyone whose name was not found written
in the book of life was thrown into the lake of fire. (vv.14–15)

If the first death comes with long-awaited hype,
the second lingers for sarcastic acclamation.

If the first death stills the heart by referendum,
the second, a televised shoot-out, ends nil nil.

Everyone feels cheated. If you say you went to
the Lesser Free Trade Hall gig – the second life's

genesis – and were elsewhere, that's a harbinger
of the second death. If home-taping was really

killing music through the eighties, the second death
is Spotify Premium. The artists eat the bullets

in monthly instalments. With Pete Shelley dead,
Piers Morgan dancing to *Promises* on GMTV

would be the second death. The Smiths' lawsuits
were first, the public mourning of David Cameron

irony's second death, Morrissey's slouch towards
louche fascism third, and fourth: the heart's

silence. Sometimes, two deaths cannot redeem
enough sadness. If *Love Will Tear Us Apart*

marked a first death, Paul Young's cover was
the second, third, fourth, fifth, sixth . . . like Jesus

crucified with every sin, he dies in me and I die
in him, in every note. If the first death arrives

when the PM tweets Happy Diwali on the cusp
of Ramadan, the second death is the hospital

chapel's empty wall of whitewash doing just
like it said on the tin. If the first death claims

the glaikit self-seekers who bounce around
the Commons like superballs on übercobbles,

or their wives off walls, the second shows them
leaning into the Styx intent on pure reflection,

blank Narcissi, practising the pseudoscience
of self-regard. Hear the mighty Fall demand

Who Makes the Nazis? They are not longhorn
as Mark thought, but humdrum breed; usually,

the second death is boredom, b'dum b'dum,
Guitar Solo! Two notes: the first sounds life,

the second death, and their resonance is left
to sing among polarities, among the clamour

of apocalypse when all will be revealed, strung
beginning to end along a still unraveling line

CHAPTER 21

He who was seated on the throne said, 'I am making everything
new!' Then he said, 'Write this down, for these words are
trustworthy and true.' He said to me: 'It is finished. I am the
Alpha and the Omega, the Beginning and the End.' (vv.5–6)

Everything is finished. It's just that the ending
is a roaming installation. I began by telling
        the truth, and drag this book to the brink
as beginnings end and ends are spun
        like God's wooden deckchair orbiting the moon;
or like the President building a thousand
        metre high wall, without exit or entrance,
around the Whitehouse, an infantillogical
        surrogate Brexit. I knew I was finished
eschatalogically and, since then, I have
        lost my bearings. Faith takes another step
along an unlit path; doubt occupies the same
        footprint. Certainty is amber traffic lights
stilling the city of mist, while everyone stalls,
        mesmerised, to watch the clouds burn up.
Everything is vanishing. A cabbage wilts
        and Russian bots revoke attempts to rhyme
with orange and, more so, with Farage.
        Farage ends, the cabbage begins; soon,
no one recalls the dense, flappy origin;
        in essence, almost synonymous; or perhaps
the cabbage plagiarized the Farage visage.
        One vegetable may hide another, just as

a plagiarist may conceal a line's source
        in Kenneth Koch by saying, 'I am making
everything new', giving no credit to God
        or Pound. I believe in imagination more
than originality. The latest candidate
        wants my vote to cage foreign children
for Christmas, to strip unelected citizens
        of heavenly citizenship, and the polls
reveal the password to victory is feeling,
        not fact. It's true, even I told a few lies
along the way, much like the first dog
        lost in space, barking mastery over
the asteroids; or Joe Totale, concealing
        his formation in egalitarian Manchester
krautrock in favour of designer label
        Orwellian tote bags. Reinventions begin
eventually to feel enough like truth
        that facts no longer prove otherwise
and reality mists over like a Brexiteer's
        deal for a Kefalonian retirement villa,
or the 19th century Haitian pirate ghost
        Amanda married and divorced last year.
Here come the latest blowhards claiming
        no one can rewrite their work quite like
they rewrite Frank O'Hara, and suddenly
        white-robed multitudes are stripping off
to try, workshop by workshop, until they
        head the hegemony and clothe themselves
in puffball. An age when saying nothing
        seems harder than detonating lies in spores

from burst fruitbodies. Fungus Trump
 on Twitter, government by beforethought,
gnome on a toadstool, his fishy hook
 deliriously flung to worms and slugs,
an absurdist burlesque. I no longer
 feel myself. I am a crude pantomime dame
permanently online, plastered with horror
 lippy to hide my grin; a product wrap
swept into the marketplace on a high
 wave that immediately dies. I ghost
Instagram Poems for zombies, beginning
 them in Poundland, and emerging fully
formed for the End of Days, when Omega
 will declare Alpha inadequately Hellenistic
and distant as history. *Everything begins
 elsewhere*, the small voice of sanity still
hisses at the Oracle of Industrial Scale
 to make its vanishing worth its appearance.

CHAPTER 22

¹And he shewed me the Public Stream of Official Discourse, blind as ink, proceeding out of the office of the HipPriest. ²In the midst, *was there* written on a tripewriter by a twatwriter, which bare twelve *manner of* tweets *and* yielded a twit every month: and the taps on the tripewriter *were* for the best interests of the British people. ³And there shall be no more parma ham: but spam shall be rampant; and her servants shall build an economy that works for everyone: ⁴and they shall see his tinyhands; and his name *shall be* enabled in their foreheads. ⁵And there shall be no mystery there; and they need no inquiry, neither light for cigarettes; for the HipPriest delivereth them stagnation and stability: and they shall be stabbed for ever and ever.

⁶And she said unto me, my gummy knife *is* dutiful and true: and the Telegraph of the Public Stream punts wearable analytics to shew unto my servants the things they must think and do. ⁷Behold, the end comes like a Nespresso pod: blessed *are* they that maintaineth the limits of aggressively marketed plastic.

⁸And I, Mackenzie, saw these things, and heard *them*. And when I had heard and seen, I turned instead to worship The Fall and other indie artist types, which shewed me their revelations. ⁹Then saith the spirit of an ex-bass player unto me, See *thou do it* not: for I am thy fellowservant, and thy brethren Mark E. Smith, Beatrice Dahl, Larry David, Clare Grogan, Denis Johnson, and all which resist the blather. ¹⁰And *a voice* saith unto me, Seal not the lips that singeth at dawn without autotune, for the time is at hand for thy dissonant melodie:

¹¹They that are unjust, let them be unjust still:
and they which are filthy, let them be filthy still:
and they that are righteous, let them be righteous still:
and they that are holy, let them be holy still.

¹²And, behold, the twatwriter tappeth its tripewriter like a heart-shaped gap under fresh attack, unhinged by Randell Jarrell's ahistorical twitch; and its praise is to each according as their trumpery. ¹³But the song of dissent riseth against the stylish purveyors of flyte, that are cast to the flayer *in* celebrity juice and dark fire: ¹⁴the mobs, and dotards, and the nonchalant *for* schadenfreude, and bodymongers, and egotists, and lit *biz*, and whosoever loveth and maketh a lie. ¹⁵And it came to pass that one third shrinketh *into* tar-studded vacancies; one third for the first time heareth the HipPriest tap arthritis on *their* hips; one third casteth their humble brags, and half truths, and Hot-100 nominations into the wine dark sea.
¹⁶I testify and my witness faileth to attract the patronage of Nationwide advertisement, and North Korean workcamp video, and Saudi Arabian CCTV. ¹⁷But let those that heareth come. And let those that are athirst come. And whosoever will, let them take the water of life freely, or *in the least* for the recommended retail price.
¹⁸For I testify unto every man *or woman* that readeth the words of this book, If thou shalt add unto these things, God shall add unto thee the plagues that are written in this book: ¹⁹and if thou shalt take away from the words of this book, God shall take away thy part out of the book of life, and out of the holy city, and *from* the things which are written in this book.
²¹The grace of our Lord Jesus Christ *be* with you all. Amen.

TWO

Bagels

I read aloud from *Priest Turned Therapist Treats Fear of God*
Tony Hoagland's poem, 'Ten Questions for the New Age',

about the friable subcultures we create to shield us from
a cut-throat world, 'the hazards of playing at innocence'.

Norman MacCaig said he wrote two kinds of poem:
one-cigarette and two-cigarette. I don't believe him,

but this was definitely a two-cigarette poem, at least in
the reading and, when I turned the page, halfway through,

you fled from the doorway and missed the ending;
the sesame bagels you were toasting had caught fire.

It was either art scuppering one of life's primordial
transitions; or life sending art a poem in fukyu form.

You never got to hear the second half of the Hoagland,
its hope that new age values might grow tough enough

to be 'successfully transplanted into the real world'.
Instead, you toasted more bagels and we ate them

listening in silence to *Money Box* on Radio 4, with only
the haziest notion of what anyone was talking about.

The Guinea Pig's Road Trip

Three hundred miles in a cardboard box carpeted
with hay, an occasional cucumber twist breaking
the guinea pig's indifference to the dominant power:
Creator of movement, Controller of water supply,
Sucker of mints, Thumb for the disembodied voice
punctuating world news with indistinguishable hits.

The guinea pig forges a path from wall to wall,
unnerved by lack of amenities. Non-events find
fresh levels of low urgency. History is being
unmade from Leith Links to Matlock Bath
as Aleppo implodes and Thatcher turns to ash.
It keeps breathing. Cottages fly by the airholes.

A Few Reasonable Examples

The shifts no longer begin with reasonable notice:
tasks unwind and shopping lists lengthen beyond
the skill set of shrinking ecological carrier bags.

Prices are up and politicians debit accounts beyond
their means, as an example to the mean, and mean
business with more than words; with sounds that bite.

The newly fat must have teeth drawn and be injected
soup on jelly plantations, according to the latest
government thin tank. Wealth care is slimming down

as an example to the needy; beds become svelte
like stretchers. Samoa Air charge by the kilogramme,
no extra for baggage, just the inner deadweight.

Is the concept too public? The scales too privately
funded? Make it simple with our everyday outrage:
I have decided to live like a cabinet minister,

as an example to the greedy, to demonstrate the vital
art of budgeting on the cakeline. A flight for Samoa
leaves tonight and my small children are paying

for two thirds of me. Next week it will be different,
the flights will no longer land in reasonable quantity.
We are bigger, wider and taller and are a drain on

our thinner resources, as an example to the under-
resourced. Is the system too baffling? Make it easy
with our guide to government the size of a chip

pickled in a chip-sized brain: you can elect to live
a less intrusive life, with limited compensation
when days no longer end with reasonable quality.

Atmospheric

The hairdressers stopped by to snip
and slice their way through the village,
arranged bouquets of missing children
during scheduled cracks in routine.

Soldiers admired the blades, waved
like stray threads at the women battling
with absence. There was no love for
enemy comb-overs even in darkness.

The soldiers chose clouds and opened
fire. As if cattle, the clouds rattled
sour milk on their mohicans. It seemed
clouds die a slow death, as everyone

resembled them after a while, falling
gradually apart. 'Atmospheric' was how
the anchorman put it. There will always
be work for hairdressers during a war.

Military

How can anyone listen to those brass military bands
for more than ten seconds? And yet some people buy
entire albums on vinyl! Today our divine celebration
is the grenade. Let us praise the humble grenade!
Hurrah! Cymbals! Contrabass! If there are deaths,
let's publicly raise the skeletons and screw our poems
to painted bones. Drown out thought with Rule Bruteania!
Sink the boats, the refugee boats! Grenades, grenades!
Poems, poems! I respect the trombonist, her broken heart
and soul. The trombonist tells me she does not trust
the soul but only goods she's seen on TV. But I know
the BBC also sell souls these days, besides their own,
by trombone, by stylophone. Those brash military bands
celebrating skeletons. Let us worship celebrity skeletons!

The Governments

Who are the Governments? They sleep in the anuses
of snails and dream until horns snap like twigs.
They crack shells, make slugs. You must trust them.
Take a mop to the slime trails. Take a mop and map
democracy as uninterrupted, oceanic greyscale:
fertile ground for aspirant tyrants, wee gobshites
who want approval, who want to be as tall as trees
and fall on your new build, on your children's children
like a biblical curse. You must praise them. You must
pin them to your walls. You thought things couldn't
get worse? Well, think again, there is plenty of slime
to be flung. They are most against you when for you.
You must sing their songs. Your voice must be heard.
Who chose the muzak? It is the governments forming
global warming. It is the milking of domestic markets.
It is a lifeline skewered by a deadline. The governments
like to paralyse the hip clubs, the happening scenes,
and perch by God's neck like cherubs, or mosquitoes.

Hyenas

You went after hyenas believing hyenas
were after you and everything you believed,
and hyenas were everywhere, feigning
lack of interest in political dogma beyond
the boilerplate, beyond awkward compromise.
They turned up wearing masks, fancy dress,
blending in with our furniture and wallpaper:
porcelain pink hyenas topped with coin-slots,
cuddly hyenas channeling inner squeaks,
hyena Barbies, hyena Kens, action hyenas
taking aim (they have you in their sights),
hyenas free inside! – with cereal packets
unopened from the 80s – digital hyenas
ripped into space, hyenas mentioned
in passing, hyenas mentioned in poems,
pet hyenas who've shaken off their collars,
carnophobic hyenas, magic realist hyenas,
Hyena Potter imprisoned in Azerbaijan,
Hobbit Hyenas, comedy hyenas who cross
the line, hyenas falsely accused of fascism
who just enjoy the country life, dead hyenas
with appetites directed at themselves,
hyenas who say Hi, hyenas who say Hiya,
cartoon hyenas, hyenas typically online,
untypical hyenas who become topical,
hyena influencers, hyena Messiahs,
hyena priests in the order of Melchizedek,
hyenas with personal hygiene issues,
hyenas in safe spaces with dead lions
pretending, hyenas for hanging other

hyenas, compromised undertaker hyenas,
HyenaXL5, HyenaTwoOh, Hyena bombs
dropped by Presidential order, J. Hyena
Prynne, Hyena Doolittle, the Oxford Hyena
of Poetry, woke hyenas as sleeper agents
for a post-liberal consensus, old white
crusty hyenas toasting red-hot poppycock,
assorted hyenas otherwise overlooked,
vegan hyenas in denial, hyenas fashioned
in God's image, long-service certificate
hyenas with trigger warnings, hyenas
sing the blues, red flag hyenas planting
you as flagpole, dog-whistling hyenas
dressed as hyena-whistling dogs, you can't
tell a hyena from a hymen these days,
every hymn ho-hums a hyena into life
if you have enough imagination, while
real hyenas – hyenas with teeth sharp
as tongues, who strip flesh and quench
the spirit – the real hyenas go about
their silent business, without reward
or sanction, taunting the dead, evolving –
always – and whether you notice them
slouching toward the Ivory Towers
or not, they will turn their eyes on you,
will think nothing of eating you alive.

Lines from Those Killed by the State

I haven't been able to poke
my nose outdoors. Do you still think
the theatre of the world is on your veranda,
admiring your absurd petunias?

Everything cracks. I am no longer I
nor is my house any longer my house.
We live, but we do not feel the land beneath us
rushing like a storm with dark wings.

No one noticed the toad in the street,
the foam on the wave, the cloud in the sky.
No one loves us like the graveyards.
Each new day gleams like an empty plate.

Truth is the shadow that will joyfully
walk on the sundial of your life,
the insect burying itself
in the rotted heart of a tree.

You can't scare me with your threats –
you clownish journalists, masters
of sponge cakes, of crucifixion.
You who live, what have you made of your luck?

~

Lines:

1. Anne Frank
2. Anne Frank, Anna
   Politkovskaya
3. Mary Queen of Scots,
   Anna Politkovskaya
4. Anna Politkovskaya

5. Osip Mandelstam
5, 6. Federico García Lorca
7. Osip Mandelstam
8. Nikolai Gumilev

9. Max Jacob
10. Robert Desnos
11. Ruqia Hassan
12. Pablo Neruda

13, 14. Max Jacob, Robert
   Desnos
15, 16. Miklós Radnóti

17. Victor Jara
18. Anna Politkovskaya,
   Victor Jara
19. Isaac Babel
20. Robert Desnos

Factory Records

'Ultimately, Factory could only have survived on sound economic principles, and it didn't have any. That was the whole charm of it.' (Peter Saville)

The leeches were living, dead and in charge,
grasping music as income and expenditure.
Thatcher's bouffant helmet was a sprayed shell
the New Romantics sidled into like crabs,
clawing and acquisitive – the novelty virtues.

Factory peddled contracts signed by drunks
on disposable napkins, fused music and art
for bedrooms. Who could forget Section 25
or Crispy Ambulance? Men in yellow trunks,
women outdoors in Spring, that's who . . .

The fans stayed indoors until Chicago House
hit the north. Property boomed beyond control:
Madchester's hottest club, gangster bouncers,
death by ecstasy, suicide, cancer and smack,
law suits, two massive bands (massive bills).

Who could forget Northside or Crawling Chaos?
Don't answer. Lapses are painful. Fourteen years
with no business plan was almost miraculous:
flowers for staff daily, the florists left unpaid.
Entertainment in spades until the charm ran out.

Basil

I water a basil plant daily. It's like having a pet
and still maintaining an irresponsible lifestyle.
Now and again I chop leaves into a Bolognese.

Now and again a plant dies. I buy a new one
because, in supermarket terms, life is cheap.
It's easier than human love, whatever that is

i.e. *whatever*! according to a school of thought
you don't hear so much of these days, *whatever*
being a sign of privilege, of not having to care:

how Prince Charles sees the world. But how
he sees the world is something I care about.
I feel it's necessary, perhaps not quite how

water feels to a basil plant, but how basil
feels to a Bolognese: a less over-ambitious
metaphor I can get behind and, God knows,

we could do with metaphors to get behind.
Or hide behind. Just as I have positioned
Prince Charles to deflect attention from me

and several dead plants I continue to water.
It's easy to offer the dead more attention
than the living: red poppies for the fallen,

ostentatious as slogans, obligatory onscreen
for those upright citizens claiming concern
for the untouchable and affected alike –

from every double meaning, they're sure
to extract a meaningless middle ground.
They march through gardens, carelessly

lopping heads from roses, and whether
they should have done apprenticeships
in horticulture is not the point; rather,

their indifference is, has, the measure
of my own. Say I surround the flowers
with barbed wire fences and gin traps;

they'll reach for their chainsaws and pitch
the tallest oak through my bedroom roof.
We'll both be feeling the lack of metaphor.

Prawn

Exit shell, larva! Enter the pelagic
    heavens to drift idle and beautiful
like an upturned boat. Consume,
    avoid consumption. Avoid clamour,
miracles. Live without a blueprint
    for survival. All you need: a degree
of luck, plankton supply, carrion,
    comfort. The last strands of humanity
print restrictions, divert nets, red
    tape the trawlers. When spaghetti
legs, pleopods, finally plummet you
    demersal, you tread fresh depths
and rise fathoms on the food chain.
    Avoid one-upmanship among stolid
bottom feeders. Admire the brutal
    grace of cuttlefish, stir-fry, cocktail.

After Epiphany

The temporary lights are dead
spots, routine illumination,
blunting surprise, it seems,
incessantly. Cars pass through
like the elephants God drives
through eyes blank as needles.
We feel sorry for the camels,
down in the humps, grinning.

Their applause falls flat as rain.
What was impossible now feels
possible and passably mundane.
The Magi brood before the stars
fade to ordinary time, to dawn
camels, to elephants of God.

The Guinea Pig's Search for God

The guinea pig has lost track of who it is or was.
It dreams of South America but always inside dark
rabbit holes which might as well be Rannoch Moor.
Minor troubles: lumps, thinning fur, the Internet's
fatal diagnosis; the guinea pig probes its bowl
for short-term solutions disguised as mark-down
parsley. After parsley, it stumbles across lemon-
scented woodshaving and social history is made.
It chews on a broccoli stem. It passes time.
Some experts believe the guinea pig probes
for God all its life but doesn't know it has a life.
It squeaks with angels. The angels hallelujah
every time the guinea pig eats the Daily Kale
and crouches silently under a platform.

Shed

There is nothing mindful about the shed's
inner darkness. I force the bolt, rearrange
cobwebs, rock the lawnmower's uncreative
yearning on a rusty hook. Everything is done
by touch, even though I come with a spent
match's urge for illumination. It is better,
I tell myself, to feel than to see; everyone
deserves a good feeling, even as it blows
like a bulb into splinters. My fragmented self
I can articulate only palindromically; once
more under construction, with the emotional
availability of a cathode ray tube television,
the one dumped in a corner of this shed,
waiting for someone to turn it on, unplugged
and out of time, electricity and language;
unmourned for, heavy as a cow in an age
of lightness. Hear me moo! *Om Om Oom* . . .

Golf

Beyond Auchterarder lie swings and greens
the envy of the globe, eighteen tiny holes
I drive at for weeks only to reach purgatory
in rocks and rapids, a hereafter the Lord God
has bestowed like fleshly thorns raking at
the heart, the rough amid the remarkable
smooth talk of sporting intellectuals, which
has me believe a bunker is a bastion of
degenerate phenomenology, an eyeful of
sand in a world of grain, usually kicked
deliberately by some bully with a 5-iron
and girlfriend caddy, her breasts shaped
like beachballs, nipples like burst balloons,
his pecs bunched in a polo shirt the size
of Gleneagles Hotel. Nothing makes him
cool though, not his x-certificate tomato
cardigan, not his inheritance the Lord God
reduced to a hundred broken drawbridges
and empty, fruity mausoleum, otherwise
known as the clubhouse, where I admire
the latest brood of buff cocktail parasols
he arranged for glamour in the absence
of beauty: no holes in one, no below-par,
thumping wood-to-nothing, no Lord God
who can't be explained in language straight
as a ball's flight beyond the nineteenth tee,
beyond curved putt, beyond Auchterarder.

Resurrection

Many competing interests seemed to be arrayed
against us but at least we had the resurrection
when the graveyards and crematoria collapsed.

We countered their promise of instant repair.
In catacombs between the Port O' Leith bar
and Albert Street, we proclaimed uncertainty

a virtue and plotted to overthrow the Dinosaurs
of London whose dour power and wonky views
could not disguise essential conventionality

and rigorous enforcement of the inessentials.
We spat out Tranströmerian creeds of *perhaps*
with theatrical apocalyptic aplomb, bubblegum

religion bursting at the banks of power houses
dumped by the Thames. We were communists
to the right-wing, the most dangerous oafs

in Britain to the safe and placid brains who ran
amok among themselves with unbridled fear of
imagination: one wanted to supervise the state,

pint glass in hand – a government of drunks;
another canvassed focus groups in invisible ink.
We sang hymns to hobgoblins and foul fiends

with satirical intent; they didn't get it, couldn't
recognize themselves behind their natural spin,
couldn't fathom how a man nailed to a cross

could be suffering or be declared unable to work
in light of resurrection, or how the resurrection
was dark work hidden from the monotonously

bland, the know-it-all blind. We saw emptiness
and it filled us like third-day bread, like a roll
of stones from tombs, into which we stared

and saw the angels rifling through emptiness;
we saw the wine stains, the body crumbled
to dust and mist, and we were not afraid.

Lines of the Drowned

Why do you have to make it be *about* something,
the present world? The most beautiful thing is a victim.

I don't think being a movie star is a good enough reason for
existing half-remembered, Hollywood's psychic dustbin.

I want to be ripped apart by music,
the thud of a great beast stamping.

All I need is a big surfboard and a piano;
the sea will drum in my ears.

The whole world is muddy. I alone am clear.
Drunk, I rise, and approach the moon in the stream.

God had blessed me. I will taste no other wine.
Water rattles that stinging coil, rehearsed hair.

Lines:

1. Albert Ayler
2. Ozamu Dazai
3. Natalie Wood
4. Jeremy Blake
5. Jeff Buckley
6. Virginia Woolf
7. Dennis Wilson

8. Virginia Woolf
9. Qu Yuan
10. Li Bai
11. Whitney Houston / Percy
Bysshe Shelley
12. Hart Crane

Bubble of the Drowned
written with Tessa Berring

God rattles 🐟 half-remembered

dustbin victim 🐟 🐟 🐟 moon sea water

surfboard 🐟 world why ? 🐟 the present *about*

my stinging half 🐟 moon sea water 🐟 drunk blessed

Most remembered sea 🐟 don't do 🐟 Hollywood's thud

big ears my big ears I music 🐟 you moon sea water beautiful

surfboard think God rattles 🐟 The rise I 🐟 🐟 rehearsed being psychic

world the great beast 🐟 make a movie 🐟 🐟 *about* taste approach

whole dustbin *about* something 🐟 moon sea water piano

surfboard star coil victim want be no sea I wine 🐟 *about*

Good stamping! I am God rattles present reason 🐟 🐟

drum a*bout* 🐟 muddy 🐟 🐟 rehearsed hair

The world 🐟 taste 🐟 🐟 is clear.

Anagram of the Drowned
written with Tessa Berring

"The most beautiful thing is being muddy. Typing the moon had me ripped apart in a dustbin and drunk by the present world. Why do you have to make it a movie star victim? A surfboard is a good reason for stinging, anyway, a stomping beast is enough to read the blood of God, I AM, existing. I don't think, I approach the abyss, taste no other wine. I will that the sea be blessed. All will be clear, is a rehearsed piano, psychic drum about something, I want great music, the whole world rattles in my ears."

Two Hearses

We waited by the cemetery gates for the hearse
to steer the curved path between stones, slowly,
caught behind a second hearse whose driver took
all pace out of living and dying at every corner.

The path was narrow as all pathways leading to
and from an after-life must be. A straw of smoke
flounced from the crematorium, the open graves
were throats about to burst into silent levity.

One empty hearse and then another breached
the gates which separate the dead and dying.
We got on board, ready for home, queued at
the temporary lights, two hearses waiting for

what seemed like an age for change to come
on wide roads flanked by cones and industry,
by dying bodies crossing to and from kerbs
in search of somewhere to stall and rest.

The rest never happened: the dying passed
over to temporary life, much rejoicing followed;
the two hearses waited for the lights to change;
nothing was the same, not even for a second.

The Guinea Pig in Crisis

The guinea pig feels unclear whether it is rodent
or mammal. Either way, aspiration is marsupial,
a fistful of dandelion leaves all it takes to eke out
a hop and skip, its mouth a twitching pocket.
It runs circles around the Australia of its cage
unselfconscious over evolution or revisionist
histrionics or Adam dubbing it a shrunken boar
(perhaps 'bore'?). Just as well it lacks theological
imagination and knows no anger, only placid
confusion. Days come to pass complicatedly:
eat, shit, shit, eat, eat, shit, shit, shit, eat,
like morse code bleeping out. . .what? Nothing
makes sense any more, even the red tunnel
seems intercontinental – from broccoli spear
to water nozzle – the length of a soul's drift.

The Future

At times we wondered where emerging Scottish poets went
between tweets, but we soon learned not to ask questions
affecting personal security. They'd find ways to keep body
and soul together if we shut up: they'd caterwaul hymns
to hospital patients for half a crown an hour. Why don't
we update units of time like we update units of money?
An hour should be an anachronism by this time. If poets
were paid according to what they're worth, the literary
economy would flatline, leaving arts cash to manufacture
the four nuclear submarines politicians keep promising,
a writer-in-residence for each. Doncha see the future
brightening like a golden sunset? The future is in capable
hands, between tweets. Headlines are a kind of poetry,
that's what we think. Shut up, everyone says, you don't
know anything, you just think things. Poetry collections,
they know, are a dying medium. Except, we think, for
those who read them. No matter, check out the new
dot-to-dot sonnet spray-painted on a dying leopard.
The neon pink of a baboon's backside is a kind of poem,
doncha know? Check out the Higher English syllabus,
my ode to missile loaders. Oh, I'm so excited! Emerging
Scottish readers are the latest anachronism, between
updates. Why aren't people allocated celebrity status
just for reading a lot? Spoken Word is a kind of poetry,
that's what they know. Doncha wish the future was hot
like poetry? We watch it brighten with a flash and bang.

The Swami

We waited for the Swami's predictions
to come to pass, and for the passing
of the Swami, resolute only in our
irresolution. The clocks were ticking
but suddenly fell silent and digital;
truth and lies mingled like insouciant
speed-daters. The Swami died years
earlier than promised and we spent
a hollow era burying his prophecies
beneath an rootless waste of ink
until budding autodictats unearthed
new reasons to believe them – simply
old reasons latterly passing through.
Are recycled gods still endlessly God?
the Swami liked to ask, liked to ask
a little too much, as if the question
implied a series of freshly aimed eggs
interrogating a bulbous forehead.
We never could tell what vagaries
were coming our way, which made
being around the Swami restorative
and yet tending towards vacancy.
It was hard enough to keep up with
bare facts, let alone what no longer
excited theologians. We were caught
between popular and expert opinion
and neither seemed sufficiently true
or attractive to heal the soul-shaped
gash the Swami notched in our sides.

The Arse

Everyone was talking about the arse.
Everyone talked in broken similes:
the arse was like no arse ever, like,
talked about. Everyone lit phones

like lighters, which hovered over
the arse to manifest light, dark,
like, to everyone. And everyone
talked to themselves when talk

stalled and online shitstorms
fell to average levels. Everyone
saw the arse onscreen. Everyone
hoped to see again the arse

they had just been, as no one sees,
like, everything. Everyone walked
the talk about the arse. Everyone
unliked their likeness to the arse.

To Be John Knox

was hard in the sixteenth century.
Now all you need is a hipster beard
or centrifugal rhetoric to appear
a force in the world. Or a victim.
Nineteen months in a prison galley
did not arouse the sweet tongue
ladies-in-waiting counted on:
'You are beautiful. Your beauty
won't travel beyond the grave' –
Knox's finest shot at flattery.
There has been flattery: a band,
The John Knox Sex Club, could be
flagged as a tribute act. Scotland
usually sidelines revolutionaries,
continues to give an affirming No
vote to Knox, never a Yes man,
who loved England and prayed
for union. Love was unreciprocal,
unconsummated. But there was
consummation. Cardinal Beaton
had ten children, doubtless virgin
births, before his assassination;
Knox's daughter married one
of Rizzio's killers. Between love
and death was a too thin line;
Knox preferred to deal in chasms.
There was disapproval: standing
for communion, proclivity to parrot
prayer books, Popes confused with
cheeseburgers, dancing, queens –

blame Knox, unlikely therapist
on whom to offload Scottish
niche perennials: difficult-to-like
wha's like us brigades, blottoed
sectarians, the misty women
conjuring summer rainclouds
from fish shops in Fife, bullied
adolescents with London accents,
the twenty percent Tory voters –
blame Knox: witty, intransigent
iconoclast. Let's nail accusations
before the High Court carpark.
There he lies beneath berth 23,
powerless under a Mini Clubman.

The Experimental Guinea Pig

Lab rat, genetically modified mongoose,
obedient brain; the guinea pig's trinitarian
contribution to lightweight scientific trivia:
it sniffs blue flowers on Bunsen burners,
proves cola submersion can strip a coat
of pelt, dodges clouds in Hotel Ammonia.
Its suffering is almost noble, is sacrifice
according to anthropocentric theology.
It doesn't know what forgiveness means.

The Popular Vote

Before the rush, their stock was dwindling,
disapproval rose to an all-time high, but now
everything is popular again, even the army
of December lawnmowers, even their sheds

and adverts for sheds. This winter, artificial
grasses grow like rumours, and night-moths
butt heads on lamps that buttercups had lit
across the moors. If brightness makes me

feel safe, I'll remember that oligarchs fall
under public scrutiny only when streetlights
are extinguished or when snowflakes turn
their dark side towards me like moons.

You don't believe me? The truth is a mist
within the sun's fixed gaze. What you think
won't happen will happen. I will be working
off my undeclared debts until, bankrupt, I

become a president. Tax inspectors uncover
billions of miniature cities between Munros
invisible to the naked eye. They exist only
as facts-in-construction until collateral facts

assert otherwise. A semi-educated populace
needs meta-fiction to survive. I'll find food
on the fly, spend winter under the labellum
of self-deficiency, which sucks! There's little

goodness in me: a deficit of vitamin, bran,
acumen and brain. As ever, I desire abilities
I can't retain, like an insect set to liquidize
fine *coq au vin* with its own spit. I spend

a fortune on implements and neglect them.
Possession implies power, but apathy walks
elections, has the biggest mouth, the most
flimsy hosepipe. By popular vote, I get what

I serve, but I don't always *get* that. 'Be
afraid!' the houseflies buzz like defective
light bulbs until I fear the might of squidgy
bodies and balloon heads, plans to ban

a free press – rolled-up, laid flat, digital
or two-dimensional – and to champion it
simultaneously. If confused, remember
everything is out there, perfectly clear.

Tools

Damián Ortega exhibition, The Fruitmarket
Gallery, Edinburgh, August 2016

The clay hammer shattered on the nail,
the nail fell, the framed watercolour
met the laminate floor. A clay hammer!
Art is useless for making anything stick.

I had a city to build before nightfall.
Damián had lent me his clay toolbox,
his clay kiln, his clay mobile phone;
I dialled to make nothing happen.

Like everything, rainfall in August was
at record levels. I prayed to the divine,
omnipotent potter, 'Stop the rain! Fire
the pots!' My city mouldered into mulch.

The mulch melded into my reflection
in record time. It was art. I called it
Self-Portrait as a Tuna Melt. I took
Damián's clay spoon and stirred it up.

It takes a tool to make art, I thought.
'Bullshit!' God said. 'Everyone knows
it takes art to make a tool, and you
are a tool.' I'm a clay art hammer,

a clawless model within a glass case,
heart of a toy, but called into service
by hardheaded nails. When I shatter,
everyone shatters right back at me.

The Guinea Pig at The Fruitmarket Gallery
during Phyllida Barlow's 'Set' exhibition, summer 2015

Tottering piles of planks! Paint-splattered cardboard
at improbable angles! The guinea pig has never known
such static contingency, such resistance to collapse
among the already collapsed. It owes its life to fear
of sudden movement, intricate shifts, cul-de-sacs.
It complains of an irresponsible lack of balance
between boulders, between choices. The guinea pig
has significant doubts over risk-free concepts of
stability. One twitch of a nose and a galaxy somewhere
sparks into quarks. It scents danger over light years of
darkness.
        In the gallery café, Imogen froths flat white
artworks; Ed's beard, symbol of bacchanalian glamour,
stirs to independent life. Iain cements his reputation
as a magnet for beautiful women. If things appear on
the slide, they hold true at root. If Edinburgh drinks
itself upright, the guinea pig will nudge it slantwise.
No matter how quietly it sits within the red tarpaulin
bodybag, the city will never feel quite quiet enough.

Alarm

Either you are getting old or the green leather
    sofa makes you too comfortable
        but dreams come easier than before.

You can't dream at night so dream by day instead.
    The bottle of Absolut will still be waiting
        when you wake, the house will still be
empty and warm. You worry that the bottle will somehow
    walk away and take the warmth with it.

All the best television takes place by night, you think,
    turning away from the alarm to another
        disturbance and this one is silent as glass,
silent as that bottle of Absolut deep in the fridge
    that's getting easy and empty and too final.

All the best dreams take place when you'd rather be
    awake and taking the warmth from the house,
        the night from the old television
deep in the room. The sun falling on green leather
    will walk away and take your comfort with it.

Either you are becoming too empty or the final bottle
    of Absolut makes you worry too much,
        but dreams are more like televisions than before.

Malbec

High altitude ensures quality in Argentinian Malbec.
I put it to the test, drink upstairs while watching
quails become startled and rise like helicopters,
bumping their heads on mesh ceilings. The Malbec
is packed with deep ruby tannins. Acid is rising to
my throat. All this ascension talk stuns the quails.
Alone among the wild birds, they swallow Malbec
and drunkenly lay eggs at random points along
the gulch. Unlikely, you think. They eat hemlock,
cause kidney failure when I eat them with Malbec
heavy in my glass. Unlikely, but true. Or would be
if there were lethal quails bumping on more than
my skull's roof. You can take or leave the Malbec.

Positive Noise

The onus on me was to trigger positive thinking.
It was hard to tell so many lies, but I kept at it.

I kept telling everyone they could do it if only . . .
My idea had the crumbling body of a Big Cheese.

Its stench floated stone tablets down a mountain,
in God's name, from one grain of sand to another.

I kept telling everyone they could do it if they were
told what *it* was, if they were told to take a telling.

I told my future self what to do with his smugness,
and felt like a king plotting how to bring him down.

My humble brags were like a jockey taking credit
for the favourite's collapse at the final hurdle.

I fed my insights into a soft-boiled yolk forty times –
like Google Translate with a toast soldier platoon.

I emphasized the maintenance of European-ness
in Yorkshire Puddings to a post-European détente.

I had feelings in proportion to Dairylea triangles
processed with a percolating mind of ricotta.

My opinions had the stability of government by
hermit crabs in search of a boulder to die under.

Imagine the best version of yourself, I suggested.
If not good enough, you need a sense of humour.

I made my name with the body-of-butter diet.
Marketing is enthusiasm transferred to the client.

My slogans had the dramatic façades of buildings
made of full-fat milk, stood grimly to attention.

Walking in St Andrews, March 2014
(for Tishani Doshi and Gabeba Baderoon)

after Ruth Stone

The hours steal every moment;
I take a photograph, Tishani's hat
shadows her eyes – a monument.
Do the hours steal every moment?
The moments are always beginning.
They are always beginning, the old
undercroft lane admits the sun's
cold blaze. Gabeba and I split
a filled baguette and a form
of sacrament is reborn from it.
The hours steal every moment:
yellow tablecloths, shop window
cake displays, works-in-progress,
yesterday's binned kebabs, new
formations are always beginning.
Near the shore are gravestones
the living glide past like ghosts –
who are the hosts, who the guests?
Epitaphs document our running
from stone to stone, glint to glint.
The hours steal every moment.
The moments are always beginning.

Journey

This is the 21.51 train from Hyndland to Edinburgh.
The hospital has a B6 ward on the third floor.
The station before Drumgelloch overlooks an Aldi.
When I eat a McDonald's burger, I eat death, I summon death.
This is not my truth or your truth but certainty.
I will reach Waverley station at 23.21.
A station whose name I can't recall overlooks an ASDA.
When I eat the Marks & Spencer falafel and spinach wrap, death is near.
If I believe the train will crash, arrival is a bonus.
The only reason to rejoice is if an outcome was uncertain.
The body in the hospital, small and cold and quiet, was my father.
This is certain, this is truth, but the last thing it feels like is certainty.

An Ending

Seeing as things have to end,
they may as well end like this:

black cats scratching perfectly
invisible glyphs on darkness

until something drops and seasons
a new communiqué rushing in

and out again; a high-speed train
dragging its utterance through

barren rural stations, unstaffed,
expecting only the Son of Man's

triumphant fall from heaven,
and instead the ending falls

without drama, utterly without
aspiration, between great cities

celebrating an unjustified
importance among themselves,

while film crews stream the signs:
fireworks, celebrity endorsements

of earthquake, war and pestilence,
Armageddon in village chippies,

and few keep tabs on the train
pulling in or pulling out without

fully stopping, a sentence of carriages
unbroken from station to station,

governing syntax imperceptible as
a black cat snatched by darkness

which, seeing as things have to end,
may as well end like this:

The Line

I crossed the line
        in days of hunger
     of plastic straws floating on oceans
     of sleeping bags burning at shopfronts
     easy pickings diminishing returns
I took my ration like an ungrateful child
        and crossed the line
to revelation its strange
corruption of evil the line
        between corrupt
and correct as thin as the line
that teases the Kingdom of God
from Kingsknowe
        the unmet expectations of applause
from plausible demands
        racism
from razzmatazz I crossed
        the line from Dado
to Dada the once experimental
now conventional from Smith
to Smythe from surreal
        via sense
in varying degrees to Surrey in summer
I crossed the fractured line   from The Fall
to Rock Follies and never looked back
nostalgically again at manufactured eras
like OasisBlur
        when Pulp ruled from Slavia Prague
to Sparta from FC
        via Inter to AC

            a new love's electricity
short circuit body on
                        the line from naked
to knackered within seconds
of drunken fondling the damaged line
                to fondness I crossed from
root via routine
            the infinite route
from ravel to ravel cleave to cleave I crossed
the line of meaning not meant
            where definition dresses in white
            noise not bad language
            but language used badly
clarity sent back to where it came from
I crossed the line
                from theological apologetics
    to thoughtless apology
            for wrongthink the thoughtpolice
satisfying some, causing others
to smear their bodies and minds
                        with anthrax
and outrage and from outrage
to anthrax I crossed
            another line
                        another line
to absolutes
            shifting in sands
from monuments to trivial pursuits
        wordgames gunplay
                    invisible lines

                    I crossed
while the powerful and censorious set up
sitting ducks to shoot at from low-speed trams
    Gaelic road signs imaginary Sharia zones
                              anything minority
crosses the line
                    from lout island's inner commons
chamber of yobs flat champagne knobs little nibbles
those preening daisychains along the dozy rows
where the line is redrawn
                         and redrawn every day
the same way dawn draws night from morning I cross
the line from good advice
                         to immersive drift
I'm a broken reed between banks between
crossed lines brassy monologues rhetorical designs
on the benefits of wholesomeness
or (*was it?*) the elegance of homelessness
austerity as aesthetic principle
                          I've lost my capacity
for surprise the most ethnically diverse
right-wing cabinet in history have problems
digesting ethics they hate
the poor   love the poverty I crossed
the line to celebrate
                         a can't-do spirit
                         blunderbuss generator
incompetence may yet save the robust
        offended by subtlety offended by directness
who jampack cupboards

a year's supply of tomatoes in tins
                    mothballed anchovies
in days of hunger
            I crossed the line
a freight train tears down bearing gifts
        fly-sprayed fruit unaffordable insulin billowy chickens
glazed scarlet as killer nightclub frocks
        and I wave it by
swaying a little as the thought overtakes me

Notes

Several poems in the Revelation sequence contain phrases which allude to lyrics and song titles by The Fall, and other bands now and again.

p.8 Chapter 4: Brighten the Corners is the name of an album by Pavement.

p.10 Chapter 5: a cento of quotations from Revelation chapter 5; The Seventh Seal (1957), directed by Ingmar Bergman; The Golden Bowl by Henry James.

p.16 Chapter 9: 'Plus ça change, plus c'est la même chose' (Jean-Baptiste Alphonse Karr, 1849) – the more things change, the more they stay the same.

p.29 Chapter 13: Simeon the Stylite was an ascetic prophet who lived on top of a 15-metre pillar near Aleppo for 37 years. People would gather at the bottom of the pillar and raise food to him using ladders and pulleys. He died in 459 a.d.

p.38 Chapter 19: slightly messed up excerpts from the Communion Liturgy of the Church of England mixed with direct quotations from Revelation chapter 19.

p.39 Chapter 20: 'the Lesser Free Trade Hall gig' – a legendary 1976 Manchester gig featuring the Sex Pistols. Many key members from the punk/indie scene claim to have been there but only 35 people were really present, including Buzzcocks, Morrissey, Mark E. Smith, the journalist Paul Morley, and two members of Joy Division.

p.42 Chapter 21: 'Everything is vanishing' – refrain from Alexander Hutchison's poem, 'Everything', from Bones and Breath (Salt, 2012)
'One vegetable may hide another' – Kenneth Koch's poem is 'One Train May Hide Another'.

p.43 '19th century Haitian pirate ghost/ Amanda married and divorced last year' – Amanda Teague, a 45-year-old Irish woman, did indeed marry and later divorce the ghost of a pirate in 2017–18.

'*Everything begins elsewhere*' – title of Tishani Doshi's second collection (Bloodaxe, 2012)

p.45 Chapter 22: 'written on a tripewriter by a twatwriter' – the critic Randall Jarrell memorably wrote in a review that a certain poetry collection gave the impression 'of having been written on a typewriter by a typewriter'. Some phrases in this poem are verbatim from Revelation chapter 22 and others are direct quotations from the UK Prime Minister's Twitter feed.

p.58 Lines from Those Killed by the State: a cento.

p.70 Lines of the Drowned: another cento.

p.90 Walking in St Andrews, March 2014: this poem follows a similar form and rhyme scheme to Ruth Stone's 'Train Ride'.

p.94–97 The Line: the lines 'not bad language/ but language used badly' is a paraphrase from an interview with James Kelman. I can't locate the interview, but the original phrase was something like 'There's no such thing as bad language, only language used badly.'

Thanks and Acknowledgements

Some of these poems or earlier versions of them appeared in: *Adjacent Pineapple*, *Atrium*, *B O D Y*, *Coast to Coast to Coast*, *Finished Creatures*, *Glasgow Review of Books*, *Gutter*, *Marble*, *New Boots and Pantisocracies*, *New Walk*, *Poetry Salzburg Review*, *Well Versed* (The Morning Star).

'After Epiphany' was commissioned by the StAnza International Poetry Festival 2014 and appeared in the anthology *The Poet's Quest for God* (Eyewear, 2016), 'Factory Records' in *Double Bill: Poems Inspired by Popular Culture* (Red Squirrel, 2015) and 'The Guinea Pig at the Fruitmarket Gallery' in *Umbrellas over Edinburgh* (Freight, 2016). 'Lines of the Drowned', 'Bubble of the Drowned' and 'Anagram of the Drowned' resulted from a collaboration with Tessa Berring published in *Aquanauts* (Sidekick Books, 2017). 'To Be John Knox' was published in the anthology *Scotia Extremis* (Luath, 2019); 'Lines from Those Killed by the State' was published in the anthology Vanguard #3 (Vanguard, 2019)

Thanks to Tessa Berring, James Midgley, Helena Nelson and Louise Peterkin for useful thoughts on some of the poems.

This book has been typeset by
SALT PUBLISHING LIMITED
using Sabon, a font designed by Jan Tschichold
for the D. Stempel AG, Linotype and Monotype Foundries.
It is manufactured using Holmen Book Cream 70gsm,
a Forest Stewardship Council™ certified paper from the
Hallsta Paper Mill in Sweden. It was printed and bound
by Clays Limited in Bungay, Suffolk, Great Britain.

CROMER
GREAT BRITAIN
MMXX